# mighty machines

# CARS

*Written by*
## Chris Oxlade

*Illustrated by*
## Mike Lacey

*p*

This is a Parragon Book
First published in 2001

Parragon
Queen Street House
4 Queen Street
Bath BA1 1HE, UK

Copyright © Parragon 2001

*Produced by*

David West ☆☆ Children's Books
7 Princeton Court
55 Felsham Road
Putney
London SW15 1AZ

All rights reserved. No part of this publication
may be reproduced, stored in a retrieval system,
or transmitted by any means, electronic,
mechanical, photocopying, recording or
otherwise, without the prior permission of the
copyright holder.

British Library Cataloguing-in-Publication Data

A catalogue record for this book is available from
the British Library.

ISBN 0-75254-672-4

Printed in U.A.E

*Designers*
David West
Aarti Parmar
*Illustrator*
Mike Lacey
(SGA)
*Cartoonist*
Peter Wilks
(SGA)
*Editor*
James Pickering
*Consultant*
Steve Parker

# CONTENTS

**4** What was
a horseless
carriage?

**4** Who invented the first car?

**5** Which was the first
car to be sold?

**6** Who got dressed
up to go motoring?

**7** What was a 'Tin Lizzie'?

**7** Who spoke to the driver
through a tube?

**8** Who drove a
Silver Ghost?

**8** Which car was very cheap
to run?

**9** Who went on trips in
a charabanc?

**10** Who were the
Bentley Boys?

**11** What did the film stars of the
1930s drive?

**11** Who used fast cars to
get away?

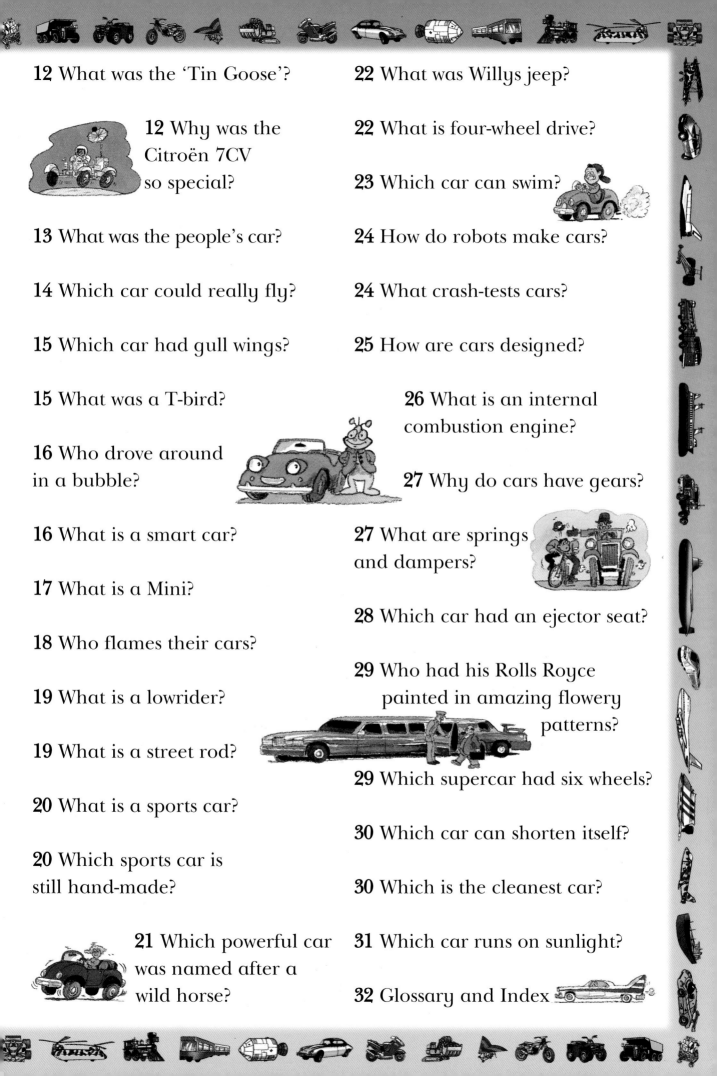

# What was a horseless carriage ?

A horseless carriage was a horse-drawn carriage with an engine in place of the horse. The first horseless carriages were powered by steam. In England by the 1830s some passenger services were operated with steam coaches. But the coaches were slow, noisy and dirty, and wrecked the cart tracks!

Daimler and his first car

# Who invented the first car?

Two German engineers, Karl Benz and Gottlieb Daimler, both built working cars in 1885. Each car had a small petrol engine to drive it.

James's steam carriage 1829

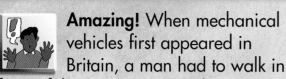

**Amazing!** When mechanical vehicles first appeared in Britain, a man had to walk in front of them carrying a red warning flag (or a red light at night). The Red Flag Law was introduced because other road users, such as horse riders, complained about the danger.

**Is it true?**
*The first cars didn't have steering wheels.*

**Yes.** The steering wheel did not appear on cars until the late 1890s. Before that, drivers steered with a lever, like the tiller on a boat, or by spinning handles on a small upright wheel on the end of a vertical pole.

# Which was the first car to be sold?

The first car to be sold was a three-wheel model built by Karl Benz. The first owner was a French engineer called Emile Roger, who bought his car in 1887. Soon Benz had a factory building cars for sale, but only a few of the three-wheelers were sold.

Benz Patent-Motorwagen

5

# ? Who got dressed up to go motoring?

Drivers and passengers of early cars had to dress up in protective clothes before driving into the countryside. Most cars had no windscreen, doors or bodywork to keep out wind and rain, or dust and mud from the dirt roads. So people wore thick fur coats or rubber capes, peaked hats and enormous goggles over their eyes.

**Amazing!** In the early 1900s, there were no petrol stations. Village blacksmiths often kept a supply of petrol to sell to car drivers whose tanks had run dry. There were no garages or mechanics either, so drivers had to carry a tool kit and spare parts in their cars, in case of a breakdown.

Model-T Ford

## ? What was a 'Tin Lizzie'?

The Model-T Ford was nicknamed 'Tin Lizzie'. It was small and reliable, and cheap enough for millions of people to buy.

**Is it true?**
*Henry Ford invented the production line.*

**No.** Production lines existed before Henry Ford started making cars. But he did invent the moving line, where the cars moved along as parts were added.

## ? Who spoke to the driver through a tube?

In some early cars, the passengers sat in the back behind a glass screen. The driver sat in the front. The passengers spoke to the driver through a metal tube to give him directions.

Austin Landaulet 1911

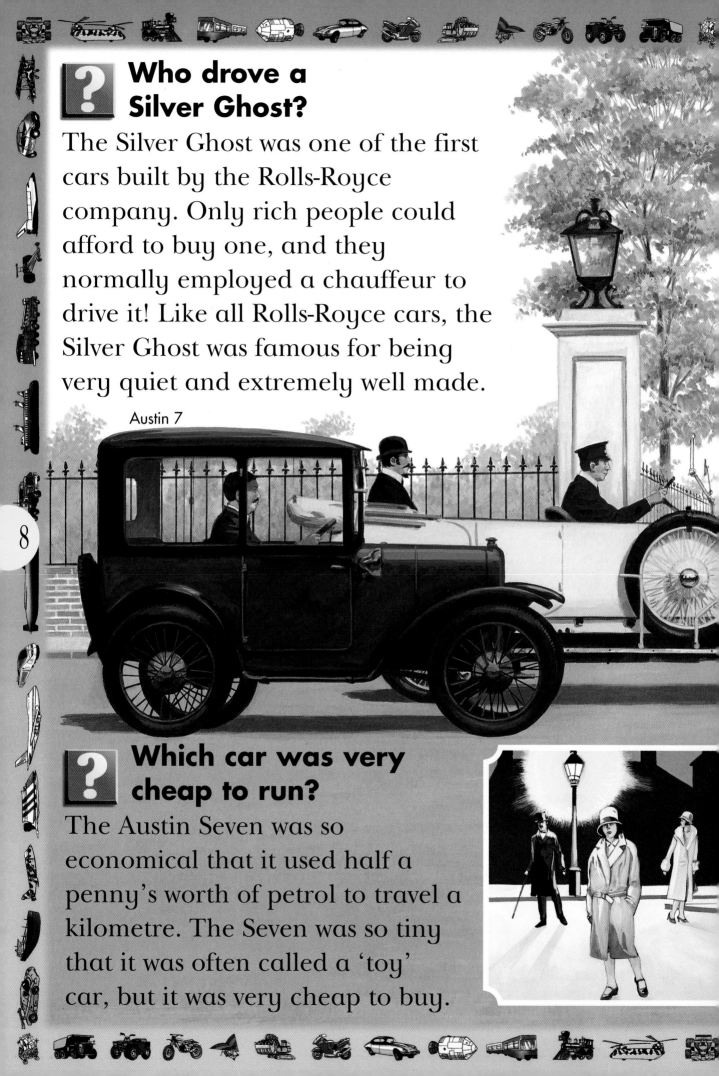

## ? Who drove a Silver Ghost?

The Silver Ghost was one of the first cars built by the Rolls-Royce company. Only rich people could afford to buy one, and they normally employed a chauffeur to drive it! Like all Rolls-Royce cars, the Silver Ghost was famous for being very quiet and extremely well made.

Austin 7

## ? Which car was very cheap to run?

The Austin Seven was so economical that it used half a penny's worth of petrol to travel a kilometre. The Seven was so tiny that it was often called a 'toy' car, but it was very cheap to buy.

**Is it true?**
*Taxis have always had meters.*

**Yes.** The word taxi is short for taximeter cab. A taximeter was a meter designed in 1891 that recorded the distance that a horse-drawn cab had travelled. When engine-powered taxis were introduced in 1907, they also had to have a meter.

 # Who went on trips in a charabanc?

Factory workers and their families used to go on days out to the seaside or to the city in a vehicle called a charabanc. A charabanc was like a wagon with benches in the back for passengers to sit on. The first charabancs were pulled by teams of horses.

Rolls Royce Silver Ghost

9

Bugatti Royale

 **Amazing!** The Bugatti Type 41 Royale was designed by Ettore Bugatti to be the most luxurious car ever. His idea was that every royal family in Europe would buy one. The car was 6.7 metres long and had a twelve litre engine. But only six Royales were ever built, and only three were ever sold. Today, if a Bugatti Royale ever appears at auction, it fetches millions of pounds.

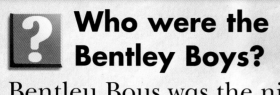

## ❓ Who were the Bentley Boys?

Bentley Boys was the nickname of a group of drivers who raced Bentley cars in the late 1920s and early 1930s. Dark green Bentleys entered all the major races of the time, such as the endurance race at Le Mans.

**Amazing!** In some early cars, passengers sat in the boot. These 'dickey seats' were hidden in the graceful, sloping tails of many early sports cars.

Supercharged Bentley 4.5 litre

**Is it true?**
*Drivers used hand signals before indicators were invented.*

**Yes.** Mechanical indicators weren't invented until 1932. Until then, drivers stuck their arms out of their cars to show which way they were going to turn. Flashing indicators appeared in the 1950s.

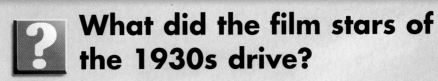

## ❓ What did the film stars of the 1930s drive?

The stars of Hollywood films of the 1930s bought luxury cars that they would look good in. They chose big, sporty convertibles so that their adoring fans could see them cruise by.

Auburn Speedster

## ❓ Who used fast cars to get away?

There were many gangs of criminals called gangsters in American cities in the 1930s. They used high-performance cars, such as the Ford V-8, to speed off after robbing banks or shooting at rival gangsters.

V-16 Cadillac 1930

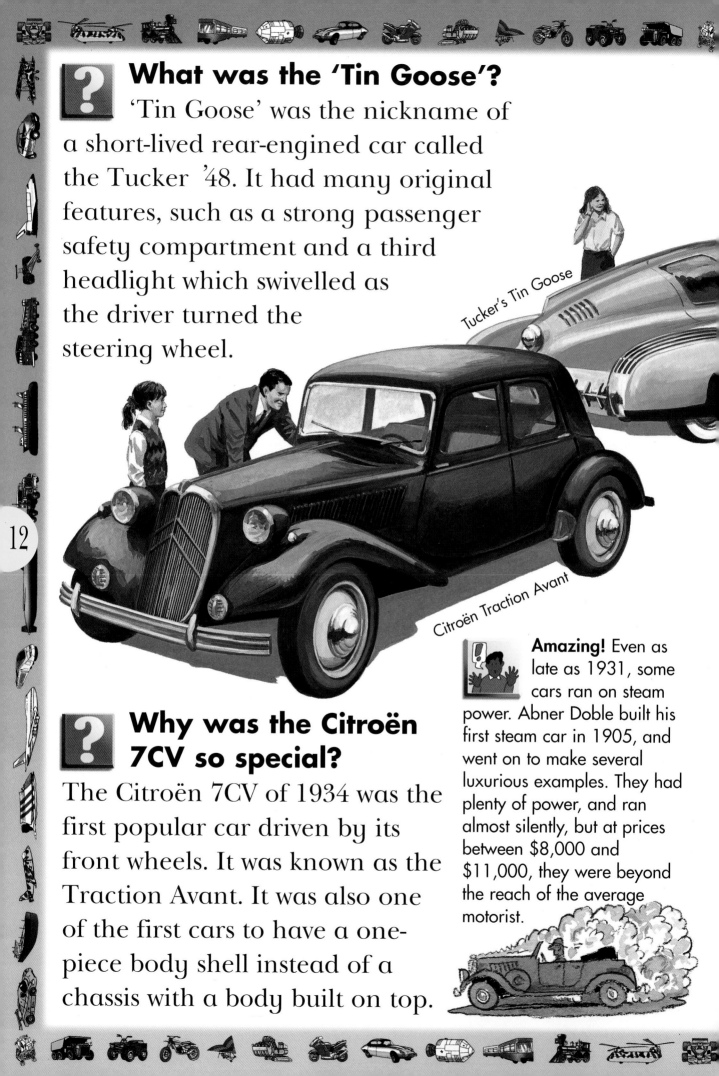

# ❓ What was the 'Tin Goose'?

'Tin Goose' was the nickname of a short-lived rear-engined car called the Tucker '48. It had many original features, such as a strong passenger safety compartment and a third headlight which swivelled as the driver turned the steering wheel.

Tucker's Tin Goose

Citroën Traction Avant

# ❓ Why was the Citroën 7CV so special?

The Citroën 7CV of 1934 was the first popular car driven by its front wheels. It was known as the Traction Avant. It was also one of the first cars to have a one-piece body shell instead of a chassis with a body built on top.

**Amazing!** Even as late as 1931, some cars ran on steam power. Abner Doble built his first steam car in 1905, and went on to make several luxurious examples. They had plenty of power, and ran almost silently, but at prices between $8,000 and $11,000, they were beyond the reach of the average motorist.

12

# What was the people's car?

The people's car was the first Volkswagen (which means 'people's car' in German). It was designed in the 1930s by Doctor Ferdinand Porsche to be a small family car which was cheap to run. It was soon nicknamed the Beetle or Bug. 40 million have been made.

*Volkswagen Beetle*

### Is it true?
*Some cars have armour.*

**Yes.** An armoured car is a military vehicle with steel plates on its body to make it bullet-proof. It usually has a small gun, too. Security companies often use vans with armour to transport valuable items or cash. Some limousines also have armour plating to make them bullet proof.

## ❓ Which car could really fly?

In 1949, American inventor Molt Taylor built a car which could be turned into an aeroplane. By 1953, the car had flown over 40,250 kilometres. On the ground, the Aerocar towed its tail and wings in a trailer.

_Airborne Aerocar_

Aerocar without wings

**Is it true?**
_American cars had the biggest fins of all._

**Yes.** In the 1950s, American car designers began adding pointy bits such as tail fins to their cars. Some features were copied from the jet fighters of the time! Tail fins often had rows of lights up the back. These huge and thirsty cars also had plenty of chrome bodywork.

**Amazing!** The driver of a Cadillac Coupe de Ville did not have to worry about blinding other drivers with his or her headlights. The car had an electronic eye which detected headlights coming in the opposite direction and automatically dipped its headlights.

14

## Which car had gull wings?

The doors on the 1952 Mercedes 300SL opened upwards like a seagull's wings. The idea was given up because they couldn't be opened if the car turned over in an accident.

Mercedes gull-wing

## What was a T-bird?

T-bird was the nickname given to the Ford Thunderbird. The first model appeared in 1953. It was a huge two-seater convertible. In the 1950s, American manufacturers built many huge gas guzzlers like the Thunderbird.

Ford Thunderbird

## ? Who drove around in a bubble?

The owners of small three-wheeled cars made in the 1950s and 1960s drove in bubbles. Their cars were nicknamed 'bubble cars' because of their rounded shape. The front of a bubble car opened for the passengers to get in and out.

BMW Isetta bubble car

Smart car

## ? What is a smart car?

The Smart car is a joint venture between watch-makers Swatch and Mercedes Benz. It's only 2.5 metres long, and weighs 680 kilograms. Its tiny size makes it the ideal car in congested cities.

**Amazing!** Some toy cars are much bigger than others! Wealthy parents can buy their children toy cars which are models of real cars. They have real engines, and the controls and lights of a real car. But they are not allowed on the road.

Morris Mini Minor

NJO 907C

**Is it true?**
*Cars can be stretched.*

**Yes.** A car is stretched by cutting it in two and adding an extra piece in the middle. The longest cars in the world are luxurious stretch-limousines.

## What is a Mini?

The Mini is a tiny British car, which was designed by the famous car designer Alec Issigonis. It was launched in 1959, and became very fashionable in the 1960s. Many Minis were bought by film actors and pop stars.

# Who flames their cars?

Painting flames, which seem to flow along a car, is one of the oldest and most popular techniques used by people who customise their cars. Multi-coloured flames give the impression of speed and power. Customising is a way of giving a car a character of its own by re-shaping and re-painting.

Lowrider

Flame painted customised car

FLAMED

**Is it true?**
*T-bucket is the name for a type of teacup.*

**No.** A T-bucket is a customised Model-T Ford with almost all of the original parts replaced with bigger, shinier and more powerful parts, such as a huge engine, fat tyres, improved suspension and massive chrome exhaust pipes.

18

## ? What is a lowrider?

A lowrider is another type of customised car. These cars look as if they've been squashed. In fact, a section of the car above the doors is removed, and the suspension is lowered.

Street rod

**Amazing!** Lowriders can jump in the air. The customised suspension fitted to these cars allows the body to be set at different heights. The suspension is so powerful that drivers can literally make their cars jump up and down.

## ? What is a street rod?

A street rod is an old family car, which its owner has customised for shows and displays. Street rods often have extra-powerful engines, a lowered roof and huge rear tyres. Really keen street rod owners spend all their spare time keeping their cars shiny!

## ? What is a sports car?

A sports car is a car designed for fast, fun driving. Sports cars have powerful engines for swift acceleration and high top speeds, plus wide tyres for plenty of grip. They often have only two seats and very little luggage space.

E-type Jaguar

Porsche 911

## ? Which sports car is still hand-made?

Morgan sports cars are still hand built at their factory in Malvern, England. Although they look old fashioned, they can compete with any modern sports car.

**Amazing!** The Austin-Healey Sprite sports car looked like a frog from the front! With its bulging headlights and cheeky smiling radiator grille, this popular classic soon earned the name 'Frogeye' after its launch in 1958.

Morgan Plus Eight

**Is it true?**
*A drophead is a term for a car with a roof that drops off.*

**No.** Drophead is another word for convertible or cabriolet. The roof can be folded back either by hand, or with an electric motor. Roofless motoring is very popular in countries with a warm climate.

Ferrari 360 Modena

Lotus Elise

21

## Which powerful car was named after a wild horse?

The Ford Mustang was named after the North American wild horse, or mustang. It was launched in 1964, and was a big hit because of its performance and low cost.

AA11 012

Ford Mustang

## ? What was Willys jeep?

Until the middle of World War Two, Willys-Overland Company made ordinary cars. But they became famous for producing one of the best known cars of all time. The Willys jeep was a four wheel drive general purpose (G.P.) vehicle, used by the American army.

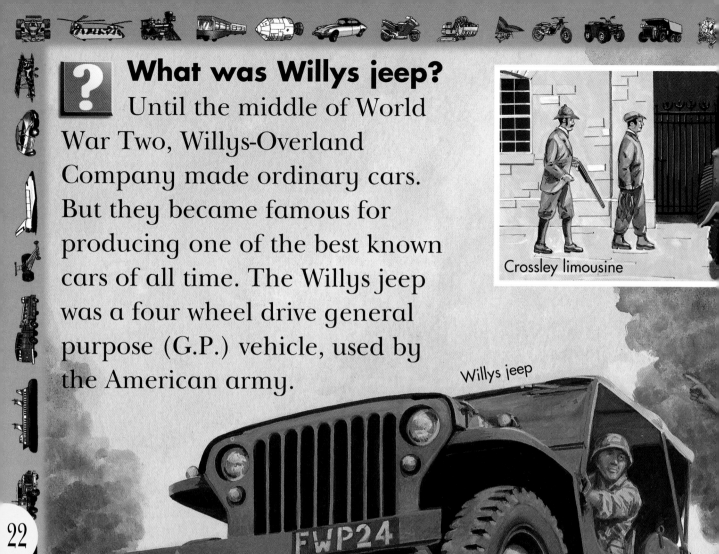

Crossley limousine

Willys jeep

FWP24

## ? What is four-wheel drive?

When a car has four-wheel drive, it means that the engine makes all four wheels turn. In most cars, the engine only turns two of the wheels. Four-wheel drive is excellent for travelling off-road on muddy tracks and up steep hills.

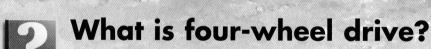

**Yes.** The missions Apollo 15, 16 and 17 that travelled to the Moon in the 1970s carried Lunar Roving Vehicles (LRVs) or Moon buggies. The astronauts drove the electric buggies around the Moon's surface, looking for interesting rocks. All three buggies are still on the Moon.

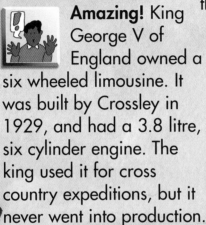

**Amazing!** King George V of England owned a six wheeled limousine. It was built by Crossley in 1929, and had a 3.8 litre, six cylinder engine. The king used it for cross country expeditions, but it never went into production.

23

## ? Which car can swim?

The 1962 Amphicar was part car, part boat. It had two propellers at the back, and the front wheels steered it, like a rudder. The large tail fins stopped water from flooding the engine.

Amphicar

## ? How do robots make cars?

Factory robots weld and paint cars on production lines. They are taught what to do by an engineer and then do it again and again very accurately. They work 24 hours a day and never get tired!

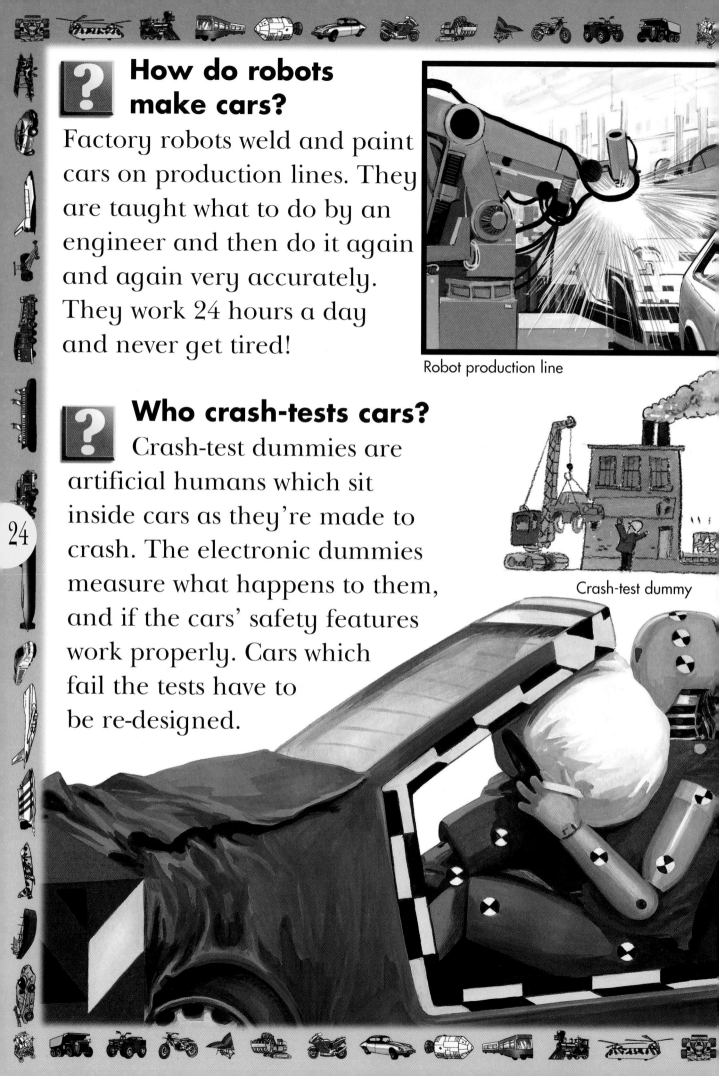

Robot production line

## ? Who crash-tests cars?

Crash-test dummies are artificial humans which sit inside cars as they're made to crash. The electronic dummies measure what happens to them, and if the cars' safety features work properly. Cars which fail the tests have to be re-designed.

Crash-test dummy

**Yes.** A wind tunnel is a tube with a huge fan at one end. Engineers check how air flows around the cars. The easier it flows, the faster the car can go and the less fuel it uses.

**Amazing!** When cars wear out they're crushed into tiny cubes by a huge machine. It squashes the car first one way and then the other. The metal in the cube is recycled to make new cars.

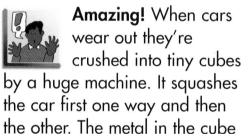

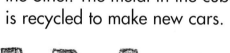

## How are cars designed?

Every part of a car is designed using computers. Engineers draw what the parts and the car will look like, and the computer helps to control the machines which make the parts.

25

1 Fuel and air are drawn into the cylinder.

2 Fuel-air mixture is squeezed by the piston.

3 The mixture is ignited by a spark which forces the piston down.

4 The piston forces the exhaust gases out.

## ❓ What is an internal combustion engine?

An internal combustion engine is the sort of engine that most cars have. 'Internal combustion' means that a fuel and air mixture burns inside can-shaped cylinders inside the engine.

Engine

Brakes

Suspension

Tyre with tread

## Why do cars have gears?

Cars have gears so that they can start off and move at different speeds. First gear is for starting off. First and second gears are for going slowly. Fourth and fifth gears are for going quickly.

**Is it true?**

*The tread of a tyre grips the road.*

**No.** The rubber of the tyres grips the road. Tread is the pattern of grooves around the outside of a tyre. The grooves let water escape from between a tyre and a wet road so that the rubber can touch the road surface for grip.

Austin-Healey 3000 Mk III

## What are springs and dampers?

Springs and dampers make up a car's suspension, which gives the people inside a smooth ride. Springs let the car's wheels move up and down as it goes over bumps. Dampers stop the car from bouncing after it's passed over the bumps.

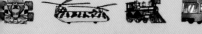

# ? Which car had an ejector seat?

In the film *Goldfinger*, James Bond drove an Aston Martin DB5 with a passenger ejector seat. Bond used it to get rid of one of his enemies. The Aston Martin also had machine guns, armour and spikes which came out of the wheels to slash the tyres of other cars.

Aston Martin DB5

**Amazing!** When the Pope travels away from the Vatican, he takes a special car, nicknamed the 'Popemobile'. The car has a bullet-proof glass dome. When the Pope goes on tours he stands under the dome holding on to a hand rail. His followers can easily see him, and he can see them, without the risk of attack.

## Who had his Rolls Royce painted in amazing flowery patterns?

The Beatles were the world's biggest pop group in the 1960s. Singer John Lennon painted his Rolls Royce Phantom VI with trendy colourful patterns.

John Lennon's Rolls Royce

### Is it true?
*There really was a car called a Chitty Chitty Bang Bang.*

**Yes.** In the 1920s, Count Louis Zborowski commissioned three incredibly fast Brooklands racing cars. The Count, a keen racer, competed in all three cars, but was killed in his Mercedes racing car in 1924.

## Which supercar had six wheels?

The wedge-shaped Panther Six was designed by Bob Jankel in 1977. It was five metres long, and over two metres wide. Both pairs of front wheels steered the car, which was never sold to the public.

Panther Six

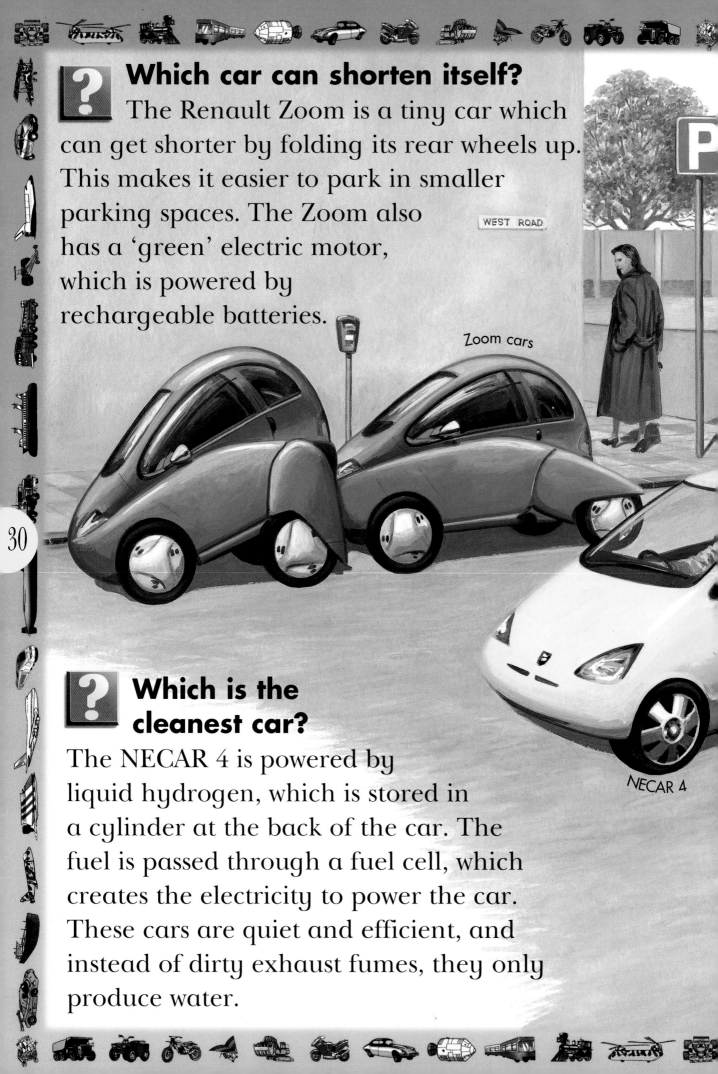

# Which car can shorten itself?

The Renault Zoom is a tiny car which can get shorter by folding its rear wheels up. This makes it easier to park in smaller parking spaces. The Zoom also has a 'green' electric motor, which is powered by rechargeable batteries.

WEST ROAD

Zoom cars

# Which is the cleanest car?

The NECAR 4 is powered by liquid hydrogen, which is stored in a cylinder at the back of the car. The fuel is passed through a fuel cell, which creates the electricity to power the car. These cars are quiet and efficient, and instead of dirty exhaust fumes, they only produce water.

NECAR 4

# Glossary

**Body shell** A strong metal shell which is the main part of a modern car.

**Chassis** The base of older cars. It supported the wheels and engine. The body work was built on top.

**Convertible** A car with a fabric roof which folds down for open-air driving.

**Exhaust pipes** Metal pipes which direct the waste gases from the engine into the air.

**Gears** Sets of cogs which transfer power from a car's engine to its wheels. By selecting different gears, the driver can start off and travel at different speeds.

**Horseless carriage** Early cars, which looked like horse-drawn carriages, but had engines instead of horses.

**Indicators** Flashing lights which tell other drivers which way a car is about to turn.

**Internal combustion engine** A machine which converts the energy in fuel into movement by burning it with air inside cylinders.

**Radiator** Part of the cooling system of a car. Air flowing past the radiator cools the hot water which has taken heat from the engine.

**Rechargeable** Describes a battery which can have its electricity replaced after it has run down. All cars have a rechargeable battery.

**Suspension** The part of a car which lets the wheels move up and down over bumps in the road. It gives the passengers a smooth ride.

32

# Index

### Is it true?
*Cars can run on plants.*

**Yes.** In Brazil there's an alternative source of fuel, taken directly from a plant. One 'petrol tree' is able to produce nearly 20 litres of fuel. The Brazilians are planning to grow huge plantations of these trees to solve the problem of increasing fuel shortages.

## ? Which car runs on sunlight?

Cars are being developed, which can convert sunlight into electricity to power their engines. The solar powered car of the future might look like the vehicle pictured below, with solar panels on the roof.

31

ecar 4

*Prototype solar car*